The Swish-Smacker Dirt Hacker

by Carolyn Crimi
illustrated by Stephen Gilpin

© 2020 Sandviks, HOP, Inc. All Rights Reserved.

No part of this publication may be reproduced, stored in any retrieval system or transmitted, in any form or by any means, electronic, mechanical or otherwise, without prior written permission of the publisher.

Printed in China.

Victor liked gadgets.

When he was a baby, the only thing that stopped his crying was the whirring sound of the blender.

"He looks so cute when he's sleeping," said his mom.

"It's a good thing we have this blender!" said his dad.

By the time he was two, Victor could take apart the toaster and put it back together again before the toast popped up.

"Did you see that?" asked his mom.

"And the toast is good too," said his dad.

On his third birthday Victor made a clock that cooked hard-boiled eggs, cleaned dishes, and swatted flies.

"That is some clock!" said his mom.

"And the eggs are good too," said his dad.

Victor filled his room with old lamps, can openers, coffeemakers, flashlights, bikes, and electric toothbrushes. They didn't work, but Victor didn't care. He liked fooling around with things.

Sometimes he took things apart.
"Oh!" he said.
And sometimes he put them together.
"I see!" he said.

As Victor got bigger, he played with bigger gadgets. He soon started making his very own vacuum cleaners.

Victor kept his vacuum cleaners lined up against one wall of his room. He made vacuum cleaners with TVs stuck to them, and others with headlights the size of watermelons. He liked to turn them all on at once. They roared like lions!

Victor made vacuum cleaners with flashing lights, telephones, and toasters. He made fast ones and he made slow ones. He made red ones and he made blue ones. He made big ones and he made little ones.

But Victor still had one problem. His vacuum cleaners did not clean very well. Victor wanted to make a vacuum cleaner that could clean better than any other vacuum. He wanted to make one that could suck the clouds right out of the sky and clean the leaves off the trees.

Victor's dream was to make the best dirt stopper and lint smasher on Earth.

"Mom, Dad," said Victor one day, "I am going to invent the world's best vacuum cleaner."

Victor's mom and dad smiled at him.

"That's nice dear," said his dad.

"Don't forget to do your chores first," said his mom.

Victor told the big kids who hung out at the playground his plans too.

"How's a little kid like you going to do that?" said the biggest kid.

"It'll never happen," said another big kid.

"You should just forget it," said another.

Victor could tell that no one believed him.

"I'll show them!" he said.

Victor went to work right away. He stopped by all the best junkyards, gathering the parts he needed. Once he had everything, he started to make his vacuum cleaner. He locked himself up in his room, and he hammered and nailed and sawed and drilled.

The first vacuum cleaner he made sputtered and choked before dying out.

"Better try again," he said.

The next one he made just spun around and around in circles.

"Something is really wrong with this one," he said.

Then, one morning, he did it.

"This one is great!" he said.

When Victor rolled his Swish-Smacker Dirt Hacker out of his bedroom, his mom and dad didn't know quite what to say.

"It's really very . . . big," said his dad.

"Yes," said his mom. "Big and loud."

"Whee!" said his little brother.

The Swish-Smacker Dirt Hacker was as tall as Victor's room, and nearly as wide. It was as shiny as a new dime.

"Stand back!" said Victor. "I'm taking it for a test drive!"

Victor's mom and dad grabbed his little brother and hid behind the living room couch. Victor sat down behind the wheel.

"Here we go!" said Victor as he hit the start button.

Va va varoom! went the Swish-Smacker Dirt Hacker as it sped into the living room.

Victor had not expected his Swish-Smacker Dirt Hacker to move so quickly.

Zoomba zoomba zoom! went the Swish-Smacker Dirt Hacker as it sucked up bats and balls.

Garoom garoom garoom! was the noise it made as it inhaled his mom and dad's fancy new rug.

Rooma roooma rooom! it roared as dishes, pillows, spoons, vases, ties, playing cards, apples, toilets, socks, skateboards, mugs, tables, chairs, and bowls all went down its long hose and into its belly.

Victor was so happy! He couldn't believe how strong the Swish-Smacker Dirt Hacker was.

"It's terrific!" he said as he went up the stairs.

"Utterly terrific!" he shouted as he came back down again.

Then, before Victor knew it, he was out the door and heading full speed toward his mom's new car.

"Victor, no!" yelled his mom.

Victor reached down and yanked on the bright red knob as hard as he could.

The Swish-Smacker Dirt Hacker rose up from the ground just in time to miss the car. Soon Victor was soaring high in the sky. When he looked down, he could see trees and houses below him.

"Be careful, Victor," said his mom.

Victor's neighbors rushed out of their houses to see him fly by. The big kids at the playground waved their hats and hooted at him like he was a big star.

Victor waved back, which was a big mistake. When his hand came off the steering wheel, the Swish-Smacker Dirt Hacker dipped down just a little too close to Mrs. Hocker's laundry line.

"Oops," said Victor as the Swish-Smacker Dirt Hacker sucked up all of Mrs. Hocker's wet clothes.

"Oh, no," said Victor as the Swish-Smacker Dirt Hacker swooped up all the pink plastic birds on Mr. Smith's lawn.

"This is not good," said Victor as the Swish-Smacker Dirt Hacker sucked up the Fink family's swing set.

The Swish-Smacker Dirt Hacker roared up and down the street while Victor tried to stop it.

Victor yanked on the red knob, but that didn't work. He yanked out the blue knob, but that didn't work at all. Victor could not make the Swish-Smacker Dirt Hacker slow down. It was, after all, the strongest vacuum cleaner on Earth.

As it got closer to dinner, Victor began to worry. His mom and dad did not like it when he was late for meals. He knew he should kill the engine and walk home, but just then he spotted a work zone.

In the middle of the big machines stood a huge crane.

"That's the biggest crane I've seen in my life!" he said.

It was too tempting for Victor. He had to see if the Swish-Smacker Dirt Hacker was up to the job.

"This is it!" he cried as he flew toward the crane. "This is the best test of my invention!"

Victor held on tight to the steering wheel. The Swish-Smacker Dirt Hacker was speeding toward the crane faster than a train. Victor gritted his teeth as it zoomed past the other machines and slammed into the crane.

Clattika clattika clonk!

The top went down the Swish-Smacker Dirt Hacker's long hose.

Grunkity grunkity gronk!

The middle went down the Swish-Smacker Dirt Hacker's long hose.

Bockatta bockatta BONK!

The bottom went down the Swish-Smacker Dirt Hacker's long hose.

With its last bite, the Swish-Smacker Dirt Hacker lunged and bucked, flinging Victor off its back. He sailed through the air and landed on a pile of dirt.

"I did it!" cried Victor. "I made the world's best vacuum cleaner!"

The Swish-Smacker Dirt Hacker rolled over to him, purring like a kitten. Victor gave it a quick pat and then got behind the wheel. He and the Swish-Smacker Dirt Hacker started back home. When he got there, he found his whole neighborhood in his yard.

"Hooray!" they all cheered.

"Where can I get one?" asked Mr. Smith.

"Do they come in blue?" asked Mrs. Hocker.

Before he could say anything, Victor's mom rushed over and gave him a big hug. "Are you OK?" she asked.

"I'm fine!" said Victor. He looked up at the sky and thought for a few moments. "But I think what I need to invent next is a bigger and better crane."